Contents

Page

Foreword
  Max Hartwell   iv

The Authors   vii

Introduction
Gertrude Himmelfarb   1

Memoir on Pauperism
Alexis de Tocqueville

Part I   17

Part II   25

Foreword

Tocqueville's reputation depends on two great books, *Democracy in America* and *The Old Régime and the French Revolution*. The 'Memoir on Pauperism', here published with an introduction by Gertrude Himmelfarb, is an interesting example, both of his method of inquiry and of his social theory, and it centres on a very modern theme, public welfare and dependency. It was written after a visit to England, and, like *Democracy in America*, derives much of the evidence used from personal experience. Also in keeping with Tocqueville's world view, it paints a distinctly pessimistic picture of contemporary society and its ills. The article advanced a widely-held and long-standing theory, still debated by today's historians, about the effects of the Poor Laws on the English economy. It argued that the effect of public charity was to foster an anti-work mentality and to produce a demoralised and dependent working class. Tocqueville at the end of the article promises a second on remedies, but, as Himmelfarb informs us (pp. 10-12), all that Tocqueville produced was an incomplete manuscript which stopped short of any substantial suggestions for reform.

Tocqueville's *Memoir on Pauperism* was written between his two large books, and followed a visit to England which provided him with evidence for the paper to the Royal Academic Society of Cherbourg in 1835. Tocqueville was an aristocrat living in an age of aristocratic decline, which he deplored. It was also an age of increasing democracy, which he feared. He was by birth suspicious of a society freed from the guidance of ancient traditions which safeguarded the liberty of the individual by providing barriers between the individual and the despotic state. The aristocracy had been a custodian of such traditions. But he was also a realist. He recognised as inevitable and irreversible a process of democratisation which levelled social status and power, but which did not necessarily guarantee the freedom of the individual. He was, nevertheless, a qualified optimist, believing that freedom could be preserved against 'the tyranny of the majority' which threatened the dignity and value of the individual in a mass society. He saw a solution in the decentralisation of power and in the preservation of traditions that were

The IEA Health and

Rediscovered Riches No. 2

Alexis de Tocqueville's

First published May 1997

The IEA Health and Welfare Unit
2 Lord North St
London SW1P 3LB

Introduction
© Gertrude Himmelfarb 1997

Translation of the *Memoir on Pauperism*
© Seymour Drescher 1968

ISBN 0-255 36394-X

Typeset by the IEA Health and Welfare Unit
in Bookman 10 point
Printed in Great Britain by
Hartington Fine Arts Ltd, Lancing, West Sussex

the hallmarks of a civilised society. He found the example of America encouraging for there freedom was protected by the separation of the power of government, especially by an independent judiciary and by a federal structure which impeded a tendency towards bureaucratic centralisation.

It was Tocqueville's concern for the individual and his opposition to the despotic power of the state which so attracted Hayek. It is interesting to remember that at the 1947 meeting which led to the founding of the Mont Pelerin Society there was a spirited debate about the naming of a society whose aim was to revive liberalism. Hayek's suggestion, which was not accepted, was the Acton-Tocqueville Society, thus identifying the society with the names of two great liberals. His choice of Tocqueville is not surprising. Both he and Tocqueville were aristocrats and both believed that European civilisation was being threatened, by democracy in the case of Tocqueville, and by socialism in the case of Hayek. Both wanted to preserve the dignity and freedom of the individual; both feared the tyranny of the majority; both saw remedies in limiting the power of the state, and both thought that, with appropriate safeguards, freedom could be preserved.

The interest of the 'Memoir on Pauperism' is its explanation of what Tocqueville saw was a great paradox. 'The countries appearing to be most impoverished are those which in reality account for the fewest indigents, and among the peoples most admired for their opulence, one part of the population is obliged to rely on the gifts of the other in order to live.' In particular in England, the richest society in Europe, 'the Eden of modern civilisation', 'you will discover with indescribable astonishment that one-sixth of the inhabitants of this flourishing kingdom live at the expense of public charity'. In Portugal, in contrast, with 'an ignorant and coarse population; ill-fed, ill-clothed, living in the midst of a half-uncultivated countryside and in miserable dwellings ... the number of indigents is insignificant' (p. 17). Tocqueville believed that for England there was 'a single deafening cry—the degraded condition into which the lower classes have fallen' (p. 32). In spite of increasing wealth, the Poor Laws, apparently, had degraded the working classes to the point of revolution. This is very similar to Marx's theory of immiseration and inevitable revolution. Tocqueville coupled this degradation thesis with a romanticised view of pre-industrial society, writing about the 'idle comfort' of the American Indian and 'the crude and proud virtues born of the forest' (p. 18, 19). While emphasising the uncertainties of modern industrial society, he ignored the uncertainties of pre-industrial society, particularly that of famine which was omni-present in all low-productivity agricultural economies which were at the mercy of the harvest.

Tocqueville did not realise that he could have stressed the moral hazards of public welfare without accepting a general degradation thesis. The numbers of the working class in receipt of welfare by no means comprehended the whole of the working class and this alone should have warned Tocqueville against generalisation. The basic mistake in Tocqueville's analysis is to equate 'pauperism' with those in receipt of public welfare, and to ignore the absolute poverty of the whole working class in countries like Portugal. While recognising relative poverty, Tocqueville argued that socially defined poverty in a rich society was more degrading than universal subsistence poverty in a poor society. He did not give adequate recognition to the wealth created by the industrial revolution and the general increase in living standards which were its consequence. Tocqueville's view is almost apocalyptic, with its prophecy of increasing pauperism and degrading dependence. Casual empiricism, like most of the court cases which Tocqueville witnessed, makes good reading, but is not proof of universal degradation. Here Tocqueville's pessimism is unqualified.

The 'Memoir on Pauperism' has its place in the enormous contemporary literature on the Poor Laws in England, expressing a view that stemmed directly from the classical economists, especially Malthus, and which dominated the formation of the policy of the New Poor Law. Tocqueville, however, did not foresee that economic growth, largely the consequence of private enterprise, would raise all living standards, and that continuing private charity would help to alleviate hardship. He clearly recognised the moral hazard of public welfare, but too easily accepted that its consequence was universal degradation. He did anticipate, however, the problems of the welfare state that are still with us.

Max Hartwell

The Authors

Alexis de Tocqueville (1805-59) was born into an aristocratic family in Paris. He began a career in government service in 1827 and spent a year in America preparing a study of the penal system, which was published in 1833. The first part of *Democracy in America* appeared in 1835. It was a great success and established his reputation as a writer. The second part was published in 1840. He was elected to the *Académie Francaise* in 1841, at the age of only 36. His other major work, *The Old Régime and the Revolution*, was published in 1856. This was to be the first part of a longer history of the French Revolution and the Napoleonic era, but ill health prevented the appearance of any further volumes. He died in 1859 in Cannes.

Gertrude Himmelfarb, Professor of History Emeritus at the Graduate School of the City University of New York, is the author of *The Idea of Poverty: England and the Early Industrial Age*, London: Faber and Faber, 1984; and *Poverty and Compassion: The Moral Imagination of the Late Victorians*, New York: Knopf, 1991. The UK edition of her book *The De-moralization of Society: From Victorian Virtues to Modern Values* was published by the IEA Health and Welfare Unit in 1995.

A Note on the Text

The 'Memoir on Pauperism', translated by **Seymour Drescher**, appeared in his edition of *Tocqueville and Beaumont on Social Reform*, New York: Harper Torchbooks, 1968, pp. 1-27. Drescher is University Professor of History at the University of Pittsburgh. He is a member of the *Commission nationale pour la publication des Oeuvres d'Alexis de Tocqueville* and the author of *Tocqueville and England*, 1964 and *Dilemmas of Democracy: Tocqueville and Modernization*, 1968, which analyses the context of the 'Memoir'.

Introduction

Gertrude Himmelfarb

THERE IS no mention of pauperism in Tocqueville's *Democracy in America*, and no mention of democracy in his 'Memoir on Pauperism'. Yet the two themes, and the two works, are intimately related.

The 'Memoir' was written early in 1835, immediately after the completion of the first volume of *Democracy in America*. But the subject of pauperism, inspired by his visit to England two years earlier, was in Tocqueville's mind while writing *Democracy in America*. Indeed, England in general was much in his mind. Gustave de Beaumont, his travelling companion in America, said that the two had planned to go to England directly from America to see for themselves the heritage that 'John Bull' had bequeathed to his son.[1] But they had been prevented from doing so by the cholera epidemic in England. Instead, in March 1832 they returned to France, which was also in the throes of the epidemic, as well as in a volatile political situation. For a year or more, Tocqueville was distracted from the writing of *Democracy in America*, first by his desultory collaboration with Beaumont on the book on penitentiaries, which had been the ostensible purpose of their trip to America (the book was actually written almost entirely by Beaumont), and then by his involvement in the defense of two of the conspirators in a quixotic plot to overthrow Louis Philippe. (One was an old friend and the other, the Duchesse de Berry, widow of the eldest son of Charles X.)

Tocqueville had barely started *Democracy in America* before leaving France once more, this time for England. His purpose was not only to visit the country that had sired America, but also to see his fiancée, an English woman whom he had met years before in Versailles and whom he was later to marry. He arrived in England in August 1833, a year after the passage of the Reform Act giving the suffrage to the middle classes. The English had survived that political crisis with remarkable equanimity, but to a Frenchman, for whom political crises all too often took the form of revolution, the country still seemed in a perilously unstable condition. 'They say,' Tocqueville wrote to his cousin before leaving France, 'that [the English] are definitely on the edge of revolution and that one should hurry over to see them as they are now! I am therefore making haste to go to England as though it were the last performance of a fine play'.[2]

Tocqueville soon discovered that while a considerable social transformation was under way in England—the 'aristocratic principle', he said, was being supplanted by the 'democratic principle'—there was no threat of an overt political revolution such as France had recently experienced. Unlike the French, Tocqueville reported in his journal, the English middle classes did not seek to abolish the rights of the aristocracy; they only sought to share in those rights. And the English aristocracy could accommodate the middle classes because it was based as much on wealth as on birth, therefore was more open and mobile than the French. Thus England seemed to be making the transition from aristocracy to democracy without violence or civil war. The threat of revolution, to be sure, could not be discounted. 'When the human spirit begins to move in a people, it is almost impossible to say beforehand where it will end up.'[3]

After an eventful five weeks in England (including a visit to Oxford where he was more impressed by the immense riches of the colleges than by their scholarship), Tocqueville returned to Paris and got seriously to work on *Democracy in America*. The whole of the first volume (originally published in France in two parts) took less than a year. By August 1834, he was able to go off for a month of hunting, 'his rifle slung over his shoulder and his manuscript under his arm,' as he reported to Beaumont.[4] In October he corrected proofs, and the book appeared in January 1835.

Much to the surprise of the publisher, *Democracy in America* was an instant success. A first edition of only five hundred copies was followed by two others that year and several more before the publication of the second volume in 1840. It received accolades from critics as well as prominent public figures and a coveted prize from the French Academy. (But not membership in the Academy; Tocqueville had to be content with election to the less prestigious Academy of Moral and Political Sciences. He was elected to the French Academy after the publication of the second volume.) An English translation appeared almost immediately, to equally enthusiastic notices—from John Stuart Mill, most notably. In May 1835, when Tocqueville made his second visit to England, he was received as something of a celebrity.

Early in 1835, after the publication of the first volume of *Democracy in America* and shortly before his second visit to England, Tocqueville delivered a 'Memoir on Pauperism' before the Royal Academic Society of Cherbourg. (Cherbourg was a few miles from his estate.) Although it remains one of the least known of Tocqueville's writings—printed in the proceedings of the Society in 1835, it did not appear in Beaumont's edition of Tocqueville's collected works in the 1860s, and was translated into English only in 1968—the 'Memoir' was not entirely unknown at the time; there are several references to it in the 1830s and 1840s.[5]

Tocqueville may have been introduced to the problem of pauperism in J. B. Say's *Cours d'économie politique*, which he read shortly after its publication in 1828 and again, with Beaumont, on the voyage to America. The final chapter of the fifth volume of that work, on 'Public Relief', restates the Malthusian theory, according to which the population always tends to exceed the means of existence and does so all the more when a policy of relief encourages the very poor to have large families supported not by their labour but by the government. Say took this theory a step forward by formulating what we might now call the 'supply-side' theory of pauperism.

> England is the country that has most havens available to the unfortunate, and it is perhaps the one where most unfortunate demand aid. Let public welfare or private associations open, a hundred, a thousand others—all—will be filled; and there will remain in society equally as many unfortunates who will request permission to enter or who will claim it as a right if one recognized it as such.[6]*

---

*   Say noted that it was because of the enormity of this problem in England that the word 'pauperism' was invented by the English. But it was not long before that word was picked up by the French. In 1834 there appeared in France another work that Tocqueville read: the three-volume *Economie politique chrétienne* by Alban de Villeneuve-Bargemont, the theme of which is reflected in the subtitle: *Recherches sur la nature et les causes du paupérisme en France et en Europe et sur les moyens de le soulager et de le prévenir*. Formerly the prefect of the department of Le Nord which had one of the

If there are echoes of Say in Tocqueville's 'Memoir' it was his personal experiences in England that brought the problem vividly to his attention. During his visit in 1833, he had been invited by Lord Radnor, a Radical member of parliament and a Justice of the Peace, to attend several court sessions where cases involving paupers were heard. The 'Memoir' quotes at length from his journal account of the first session, recording his own impressions of the applicants for relief as well as Radnor's comments on the corrupting effects of the poor law. The law, Radnor told him, encouraged irresponsibility by making people feel that they had a right to public support, and immorality by making illegitimate children a source of material benefit to the mother, giving her, in effect, a 'dowry of infamy' (pp. 34-36).*

It was during this visit, too, that Tocqueville met Nassau Senior, who was to remain a good friend, a frequent correspondent, and a valuable informant about social and economic affairs. Senior recalls Tocqueville's announcing himself: 'I am Alexis de Tocqueville and I have come to make your acquaintance'.[7] An economist and professor at Oxford, Senior was the most influential member of the Royal Commission charged with preparing an extensive report on the poor laws. Tocqueville had seen a preliminary volume of *Extracts* published in 1833 which had aroused his interest, and in March of the following year he wrote to Senior requesting a copy of the report itself.[8] A year later, having been invited to deliver the paper to the Cherbourg Society, he wrote again asking for the text of the New Poor Law adopted as a result of that report.[9] Senior sent him those documents, with no undue display of modesty regarding his own contribution to them. 'The report,' he wrote Tocqueville, 'or at least three-fourths of it, was written by me, and all that was not

---

highest incidences of pauperism among its industrial workers, Villeneuve-Bargemont maintained that pauperism was a problem not of idleness but of industry, a lack of work or insufficient wages, for which neither private nor public charity was a solution.

* Although Tocqueville twice assured the readers of the 'Memoir', once preceding and again following the quotation from the journal, that he had changed nothing from the journal account and was reproducing it 'with scrupulous exactness', the extract does not correspond exactly to the original. The final paragraph as it appears in the 'Memoir' is a rough composite of several entries in the journal; the dramatic phrase, 'a dowry of infamy', is not in the original at all.

written by me was re-written by me. The greater part of the Act, founded on it, was also written by me; and in fact I am responsible for the effects, good or evil (and they must be one or the other in an enormous degree), of the whole measure.'[10]

At one point in his journal in 1833, speculating about the possibility of revolution, Tocqueville commented on the increased 'misery' caused by the poor laws which coincided with the agitation over the Reform Act, a combination that 'could no doubt give popular passions an impulse which it is very hard to foresee'.[11] In fact, discontent with the poor laws long antedated the Reform Act and was not, as has been suggested, part of a strategy by 'a new and self-conscious middle class' eager to wrest control from the 'landed interest'.[12] The Royal Commission itself had been appointed by the unreformed parliament several months before the passage of the Reform Act. Two years earlier a Select Committee of the House of Lords had been formed to inquire into the poor laws. This had been provoked by the 'Swing riots', a form of rural Luddism directed primarily against the threshing machines but spilling over into the burning of ricks and barns and threatening letters to landlords, farmers, and parsons (often over the signature of 'Captain Swing', hence the name given to the riots). Much exaggerated by the press, partly because of the revolution in France at the time, the riots and the subsequent agitation over the Reform Bill gave credence to the impression, shared by Tocqueville, that England might be on the verge of revolution.

For parliament—both houses of parliament—to raise the issue of the poor laws was itself provocative, for it called into question an institution that had earned England the distinction of being the first country to establish a national, legal, compulsory, public, secular system of relief. The poor laws dated back to the sixteenth century when the dissolution of the monasteries obliged the government to make provision for the indigent who had previously been cared for by the church. Toward the end of Elizabeth's reign, the laws were codified, providing alms ('outdoor relief') and almshouses ('indoor relief') for the aged and infirm, apprenticeship for children, and temporary shelter and work for the able-bodied in workhouses or poorhouses. Although the system was nation-wide, the administration was local, each parish being required by law to levy taxes (poor rates) on householders to pay for the relief of those having a 'settlement' (a legal residence) within its bounds. This system, applied at different times and places with varying degrees of rigour or leniency, survived two centuries of revolutions, wars, and momentous social and industrial changes.

A major innovation came about almost unwittingly in the late eighteenth century, in the form of the 'Speenhamland system', as it came to be called. Responding to the bad harvest of 1795 and the hardships created by the Napoleonic Wars, the Justices of the Peace of Berkshire, meeting at Speenhamland, decreed that 'every poor and industrious man' whose earnings fell below a given standard, determined by the price of bread and the size of his family, would receive a subsidy from the parish to bring his income up to that subsistence level. A similar policy was soon adopted by other counties, especially in the depressed rural areas of the south, with the result that a considerable number of labourers became dependent upon the parish.

The result was not only a considerable rise in the poor rates (which at one point came to almost one-fifth of the total national expenditure), but also a cycle of evils that was generally attributed to the poor laws: a decrease in wages (which were supplemented out of the rates), a decline of the yeomanry (who had to pay the rates), a rise in agricultural unemployment (the yeomen swelling the ranks of the agricultural labourers), a fall in productivity (pauper labour being less efficient than wage-earners), higher food prices (resulting from the decline of productivity), an increase of population (relief encouraging earlier marriages and more children), still lower wages (because of the increase of population)—all of which was said to contribute to the 'pauperization' and 'demoralization' of the poor. By the early 1830s, the demand for a reform of the poor laws was almost as insistent as the demand for a reform of the electoral laws.

The appointment of a Royal Commission is often an evasive or delaying tactic on the part of the government. In this case, it was a deliberate incitement to action. Nassau Senior and Edwin Chadwick (Bentham's former secretary who was also on the commission and who was even more energetic and single-minded than Senior) knew from the start what they hoped to accomplish and vigorously set about doing it, organizing the preparation of the report, writing it, circulating it, and publicizing it. 15,000 copies of the preliminary 400-page volume of *Extracts* were sold in 1833 and 10,000 copies of the final 200-page Report the following year. Another 10,000 copies of the Report were distributed free to local authorities, and fifteen volumes of testimony and documents were issued in support of the Report. After this barrage of argument, evidence, and publicity, it is little wonder that the Poor Law Amendment Act of 1834 (the New Poor Law, as it came to be known) adopted most of the recommendations of the Report.

Contrary to the advice of Thomas Malthus and others, the Report recommended the reform rather than abolition of the poor laws, the main purpose of the reform being to undo the 'mischievous ambiguity of the word *poor*'.[13] In effect, Speenhamland was to be nullified by sharply distinguishing between the 'independent poor' (the labouring poor) and the indigent (the paupers), who alone were to be the recipients of relief. Outdoor relief, in money or kind, would continue to be provided for the aged and sick. The able-bodied, however, were to be assisted only in the workhouse and only under the principle of 'less-eligibility'—under conditions that were less 'eligible' (less desirable or favourable) than those of the independent laborer. By this means, the able-bodied pauper would be encouraged to become independent, the labourer would be discouraged from lapsing into a condition of pauperism, and the truly indigent (to whom the principle of less-eligibility did not apply) would be cared for as they had been before.

It is against this background that Tocqueville wrote his 'Memoir on Pauperism'. Although his analysis was meant to apply to all countries, the case of England looms large in it, England being the prototype for social reform as America was for democratic government. But Tocqueville went much further than the English reformers by challenging the fundamental principle of public relief itself—of any law that establishes relief as a right.

The 'Memoir' is, in effect, a series of paradoxes. It opens with the tantalising picture of a Europe in which the most impoverished countries have the least number of paupers, while the most opulent country, England, has the most. To explain this paradox, Tocqueville (like Rousseau before him) traces the evolution of society from the prehistoric hunting stage, when men were fully occupied in meeting their most basic needs and hence were essentially equal, to the agricultural stage when the cultivation and possession of land permitted them to satisfy wants that went beyond their needs, thus creating the conditions for inequality. Every subsequent era of history had its own incongruities: the medieval period, when ostentatious luxuries combined with minimal comforts; and modern times, when an industrial economy brings with it prosperity to increased numbers of men, while the vicissitudes of that economy reduce others to the condition of pauperism. The progress of civilisation, transforming more and more 'wants' into 'needs', produces a pauper class in England that is almost rich by the standards of other countries, and at the same time gives rise to a society able and willing to alleviate the conditions of that class. Thus it comes about that the richest country has the largest number of paupers.

It is at this stage that 'public charity' or 'legal charity' (relief or welfare as we now say) begins to supplement the private, voluntary charity that was the traditional form of assistance to the poor. And it is here that we confront the ultimate irony of history: the unforeseen and unfortunate consequences of good intentions.

> At first glance there is no idea which seems more beautiful and grand than that of public charity. Society is continually examining itself, probing its wounds, and undertaking to cure them. At the same time that it assures the rich the enjoyment of their wealth, society guarantees the poor against excessive misery. It asks some to give of their surplus in order to allow others the basic necessities. This is certainly a moving and elevating sight (p. 26).

However noble in its intentions, public charity is fatally flawed, Tocqueville finds, because it denies the most basic fact of human nature: that men will work only to sustain life or to improve their condition. Unfortunately, it is the first motive that impels the vast majority of men, and to deprive them of that by giving them a legal right to charity is to condemn them to a life of idleness and improvidence. Here we are presented with yet another paradox. 'Right' itself is an elevating and inspiring idea. There is something great and virile in the idea of right which removes from any request its suppliant character, and places the one who claims it on the same level as the one who grants it.' (p. 30) But a right to public charity, unlike other rights, degrades the man who claims it by condemning him to a life of dependency and idleness.[14]

It is easy to overlook, in Tocqueville's indictment of public charity, a significant qualification, for almost in passing he explains that his objections apply only to the able-bodied. He concedes the utility, even the necessity, of public charity for 'inevitable evils such as the helplessness of infancy, the decrepitude of old age, sickness, insanity', as well as in times of 'public calamities'; at such times relief is 'as spontaneous as unforeseen, as temporary as the evil itself' (p. 37).* It is only the able-bodied, claiming relief as a permanent right, who are the problem. But even the able-bodied are not without recourse, for they can call upon private charity in times of need—a charity that does not carry with it any right or assurance but is as 'spontaneous' and 'temporary' as public relief in times of public calamities.

If the burden of the 'Memoir' is an argument against public charity, charity as a right, a corollary of the argument is a defense of private charity, charity as an act of mercy. Private charity, Tocqueville argues, given 'secretly and temporarily', is less humiliating and degrading to the recipient than public charity, which may be claimed as a right but is in fact a 'notarized manifestation of misery, of weakness, of misconduct' (pp. 30-31). Moreover, society is better served by private than public charity. Where individual, voluntary charity establishes a 'moral tie' between the giver and the receiver, legal charity removes any element of morality from the transaction. The donor (the taxpayer) resents his involuntary contribution, and the recipient feels no gratitude for what he gets as a matter of right and which in any case he feels to be insufficient (p. 31).**

---

*   Say shared Tocqueville's objection to public relief, with similar qualifications, approving, for example of *hospices* for abandoned children so long as the parents did not come to regard them as an 'ordinary resource', a kind of free hostel. He also favoured help for those whose misfortunes were not caused by their own misconduct or who had natural infirmities such as blindness or deafness; their numbers, he explained, would not increase by the relief given them. 'Humanity requires that society assist them, and politics does not preclude that assistance.' (Say, J.B., *Cours d'économie politique*, Paris, 1828, V, pp. 360-63.)

**   Tocqueville himself was a charter member of two institutions that served as coordinating bodies for private charities, the *Annales de la Charité* formed in 1845 and the *Société d'Economie Charitable* in 1847.

This is the final paradox of Tocqueville's argument. Private charity may seem weaker than public charity because it provides no sustained and certain help for the poor. In one sense, however, this is its strength, for it is precisely its temporary and voluntary character that enables it to alleviate many miseries without breeding others. But it is also a problem, for the private charity that was sufficient in the Middle Ages may be insufficient in the present industrial age. This is the question that now confronts society. If public charity is unsatisfactory and private charity inadequate, how can this new kind of pauperism be averted so that the working classes do not 'curse the prosperity that they produce?' (p. 38). At this critical point, the essay abruptly ends, with Tocqueville's promise to take up the issue of preventive measures in a paper the following year.

That sequel, announced for publication by the Academic Society of Cherbourg in 1838, never appeared, and until recently it has been assumed that it had not been written. The Tocqueville archives, however, have turned up a manuscript entitled 'Second Work on Pauperism, 1837', consisting of sixteen numbered pages and an additional five pages of insertions; a compilation of these now appears in the new edition of his collected works.[15]

The second essay opens, as the first did, with an historical survey of the problem. The growth of large farms, we are told, led to the proletarianisation of small farmers, bringing with it the familiar symptoms of demoralisation: intemperance, improvidence, imprudent marriage and many children. In France, where estates are commonly divided by inheritance, this condition is less serious than in England where primogeniture prevails, for it is the ownership of property, however small, that instills the moral and social virtues that prevent pauperism.* Unfortunately,

---

*   Senior tried, unsuccessfully, to convince Tocqueville that primogeniture and entail were not the evils Tocqueville thought them, and that England was, in fact, more democratic than France. (*Oeuvres*, VI, Pt. 2, pp. 89-90, Senior to Tocqueville, 27 February 1841.)

         In one of his notes written in preparation for the writing of *Democracy*, Tocqueville observed:

         "What is most important for democracy is not that great fortunes should not exist, but that great fortunes should not

the division of industrial property is not feasible, industry being 'aristocratic' in structure, divided between a wealthy capitalist class and a propertyless proletariat. The problem is aggravated, in England at any rate, because industry is more subject to commercial crises than agriculture. (France, being more self-sufficient and less dependent on foreign trade, is less subject to such crises.)

The question, then, is how to infuse the industrial worker with 'the spirit and the habits of property'?[16] One solution, to give the workers an interest in the factory, would obviously be opposed by the capitalists; another, the establishment of workers' co-operatives, is likely to fail because of inefficiency or internal strife. In the future, 'associations of workers' might succeed in controlling large industries, but that is as yet premature. In the meantime, other strategies might be pursued, such as savings banks run by the state, encouraging workers to save by offering them favourable interest rates; or savings banks merged with local pawnshops, enabling the poor to borrow at lower rates than are normally exacted from the pawnshops. Both, however, have the serious disadvantage of promoting an undue degree of state control and centralisation.

The manuscript concludes without resolving the problem. One can well understand Tocqueville's refusal to publish this second memoir—or even to finish it. Perhaps because the problem of industrial pauperism seemed to him intractable, or perhaps because he had not given it enough thought, this essay lacks the sweep and passion of the first. The underlying principles are clear enough: the working classes, in industry as in agriculture, need a stake in property if they are not to succumb to the vices of pauperism; and whatever measures are taken to alleviate their condition must not contribute to the greater strength and centralisation of the state. But the weakness of the essay is also

---

remain in the same hands. In that way there are rich men, but they do not form a class.

"It may be that trade and industry are creating greater private fortunes in America now than sixty years ago. But the abolition of the rights of primogeniture and entail have brought it about that the democratic passions, instincts, maxims, and tastes are more in the ascendant now than they were sixty years ago." (*Democracy*, p. 772.)

clear: a failure of imagination about the potentialities of industrialism to improve the condition of the poor without recourse to charity, private or public, or to such trivial measures of reform as lower interest rates in pawnshops.

More than half-a-century earlier, Adam Smith had anticipated the problem of industrial pauperism when he made the wealth of nations—and the well-being of every class within the nation—dependent upon a free, expanding, 'progressive' economy. It is curious that Smith is rarely mentioned in any of Tocqueville's works, and not at all in this essay[17]—all the more so because both Say and Senior, Tocqueville's mentors in economic affairs, were disciples of Smith. Even without invoking Smith, they could have instructed Tocqueville not only on the virtues of free trade and a free market (which Tocqueville favoured), but also on the virtues of industrialism, capitalism, and technology, toward which Tocqueville was either hostile or, at best, ambivalent. It is even more curious that Tocqueville, so prescient about democracy as the wave of the future, should have failed to see that industrialism was as well—indeed, that the two were inextricably intertwined. Instead, in *Democracy in America* (as in his second essay on pauperism), Tocqueville assumed that the two were essentially antithetical, the 'aristocratic' industrial sector constituting 'one great and unfortunate exception' to the dominant, essentially democratic agricultural sector.[18]*

If *Democracy in America* is still so pertinent today, it is because Tocqueville's dire predictions about industrialism were not realised. Democracy survived and progressed, not in spite of but

---

*   Occasionally in *Democracy in America* Tocqueville concedes the growing power of industrialism, as in the chapter, 'What Gives Almost All Americans a Preference for Industrial Callings'.But the following chapter, 'How an Aristocracy may be Created by Industry', explains that while the mass of the nation, engaged in agriculture, becomes more democratic and egalitarian, the industrial part becomes more aristocratic and class-divided. Unlike the old paternalistic, agricultural aristocracy, 'the industrialized aristocracy of our day, when it has impoverished and brutalized the men it uses, abandons them in time of crisis to public charity to feed them'. This aristocracy, Tocqueville says, is 'one of the hardest that have appeared on earth'—a judgment immediately (and inexplicably) qualified: 'But at the same time it is one of the most restrained and least dangerous.' (*Ibid.*, pp. 530-31.)

because of the democratic tendencies inherent in industrialism itself. Just as the Founding Fathers had sought 'a republican remedy for the diseases most incident to republican government',[19] so industrialism itself has helped provide at least some of the remedy for the diseases incident to both industrialism and democracy.

So too, Tocqueville's 'Memoir on Pauperism'—the first Memoir, at any rate—resonates in an industrial and even post-industrial society. We can see the shadow of our chronically dependent 'underclass' in Tocqueville's description of the pauper class spawned by the Old Poor Law: 'The number of illegitimate children and criminals grows rapidly and continuously, the indigent population is limitless, the spirit of foresight and of saving becomes more and more alien' (p. 32). We can sympathise, as he did, with the principle of providing work for able-bodied applicants for relief, but also with the difficulties in carrying out that principle: Is there enough public work to be done, and in the areas where it is required? Who could take the responsibility for 'determining its urgency, supervising its execution, setting the price?' (p. 29). And we can share his qualms about public authorities who have to judge the able-bodied claimants for relief. How can they distinguish 'unmerited misfortune from an adversity produced by vice'? And even if that distinction could be made, would they have the heart to act upon it? 'Who would dare to let a poor man die of hunger because it's his own fault that he is dying? Who will hear his cries and reason about his vices?' (p. 29)

We can also, today more than ever, appreciate Tocqueville's criticism of public charity as a legal right—an 'entitlement', as we now say. After fifty years of the welfare state in Britain and sixty years of the relief system introduced by the New Deal in the United States, the idea of such an entitlement is being called into question in both countries as they try to cope with the consequences Tocqueville foresaw. The United States has gone so far as to enact a major reform: the 'devolution' of relief to the states. On the surface a merely administrative measure, it has potentially momentous consequences, for it eliminates the main form of relief as a national, legal entitlement. No longer bound by the principle of right, the individual states will be free to make whatever arrangements they see fit to care for the indigent within their borders.

This reform has prompted even more radical proposals. If the devolution of authority from the federal government to the states is desirable, why not the devolution from the states to local governments? And if to local governments, why not to private institutions—charities, churches, community groups, business enterprises, mutual aid societies, and, above all, families?

At this point, Tocqueville's discussion of private charity as opposed to public relief takes on added significance, for it confirms one of the main themes of *Democracy in America*: the importance of civil society. If public relief is an invitation both to individual irresponsibility and to an overweening state, private charity, filtered through the institutions of civil society, may be the remedy for both. More than a century-and-a-half after its publication, *Democracy in America* is one of the most cited and revered documents of our time, and the idea of civil society has become the rallying cry of liberals and conservatives alike. Tocqueville's 'Memoir on Pauperism' is a worthy footnote to that document and a notable contribution to the idea of civil society.

Notes

1   Jardin, A., *Tocqueville: A Biography*, trans. Davis, L. and Hemenway, R., New York, 1988, p. 197.

2   *Ibid.*

3   Tocqueville, *Journeys to England and Ireland*, trans. Lawrence, G. and Mayer, K.P., ed. Mayer, J.P., London, 1958, pp. 59-60, 66-68, 73.

4   Jardin, p. 200.

5   The essay was reprinted in the *Bulletin des sciences économiques et sociales du Comité des travaux historiques et scientifiques* in 1911; *Commentaire*, Autumn 1983 and Winter 1983-4; and Tocqueville's *Oeuvres complètes*, Mayer, J.P. (ed.), XVI, Paris, 1989. An English translation by Seymour Drescher is in *Tocqueville and Beaumont on Social Reform*, Drescher, (ed.), New York, 1968, and was reprinted in *The Public Interest*, Winter 1983, with an introduction by Himmelfarb, G. For contemporary citations of the essay, see *Oeuvres*, XVI, p. 139, n. 23, and *Tocqueville and Beaumont on Social Reform*, p. 2, n. 1.

6   Say, J.B., *Cours d'économie politique*, Paris, 1828, V, p. 352 (excerpt trans. by Seymour Drescher, *Dilemmas of Democracy: Tocqueville and Modernization*, Pittsburgh, 1968, p. 109, n. 26). See also Tocqueville, *Oeuvres*, XVI, pp. 21-22; and VI, Pt. 2 *(Correspondance Anglaise)*, Paris, 1991, p. 36, n. 1.

7   *Correspondence and Conversations of Alexis de Tocqueville with Nassau William Senior*, Simpson, M.C.M. (ed.), New York, 1968 (reprint of 1872 edition), I, p. iii.

8   Tocqueville, *Oeuvres*, VI, Pt. 2, pp. 65-66, 24 March 1834.

9   *Ibid.*, p. 73, 14 March 1835.

10 *Ibid.*, p. 75, 18 March 1835.

11 The English translation has this as an increase of 'poverty', *Journeys*, p. 73. In French it is an increase of 'misery', *Oeuvres, (Voyages en Angleterre, Irlande, Suisse et Algérie)* V, Pt. 2, Paris, 1958, p. 43.

12 Hobsbawm, E.J., *Industry and Empire*, London, 1968, p. 106.

13 Himmelfarb, G., *The Idea of Poverty: England in the Early Industrial Age*, New York, 1984, p. 159.

14 The discussion of rights in *Democracy in America*, vol. I, chapter 6, deals entirely with political rights.

15 'Second mémoire sur le paupérisme,' *Oeuvres*, XVI, pp. 140-57.

16 *Oeuvres*, XVI, p. 146.

17 There is one passing reference to Smith in Tocqueville's notes on Say in 1828 (*Oeuvres*, XVI, p. 429), and another in his talk to the Academy of Moral and Political Sciences many years later, XVI, p. 232, 3 April 1852. (J. P. Mayer misdates this as 2 April 1853, *Alexis de Tocqueville: A Biographical Study in Political Science*, [New York, 1960], p. 90.) Smith's name does not appear in *Democracy*, or in Tocqueville's correspondence with Senior, or in his journal on his English trips, or in the first 'Memoir on Pauperism', where Tocqueville criticizes at some length the English poor law for reducing the mobility and interfering with the liberty of the poor—an argument Smith had popularized in the *Wealth of Nations*.

18 *Democracy*, pp. 558-59. Tocqueville's journal on his trip to England in 1835 contains a devastating account of Manchester (*Journey*, pp. 104-08. See also Drescher, *Dilemmas of Democracy*, for a discussion of his views on industrialism).

19 *Federalist Papers*, No. 10.

Memoir on Pauperism

Alexis de Tocqueville
Translated by Seymour Drescher

Part I

The Progressive Development of Pauperism among Contemporaries and the Methods Used to Combat it

WHEN ONE crosses the various countries of Europe, one is struck by a very extraordinary and apparently inexplicable sight.

The countries appearing to be most impoverished are those which in reality account for the fewest indigents, and among the peoples most admired for their opulence, one part of the population is obliged to rely on the gifts of the other in order to live.

Cross the English countryside and you will think yourself transported into the Eden of modern civilisation—magnificently maintained roads, clean new houses, well-fed cattle roaming rich meadows, strong and healthy farmers, more dazzling wealth than in any country of the world, the most refined and gracious standard of the basic amenities of life to be found anywhere. There is a pervasive concern for well-being and leisure, an impression of universal prosperity which seems part of the very air you breathe. At every step in England there is something to make the tourist's heart leap.

Now look more closely at the villages; examine the parish registers, and you will discover with indescribable astonishment that one-sixth of the inhabitants of this flourishing kingdom live at the expense of public charity. Now, if you turn to Spain or even more to Portugal, you will be struck by a very different sight. You will see at every step an ignorant and coarse population; ill-fed, ill-clothed, living in the midst of a half-uncultivated countryside and in miserable dwellings. In Portugal, however, the number of indigents is insignificant. M. de Villeneuve estimates

17

that this kingdom contains one pauper for every twenty-five inhabitants.[1] Previously, the celebrated geographer Balbi gave the figure as one indigent to every ninety-eight inhabitants.[2]

Instead of comparing foreign countries among themselves, contrast the different parts of the same realm with each other, and you will arrive at an analogous result; you will see on the one hand the number of those living in comfort, and, on the other, the number of those who need public funds in order to live, growing proportionately.

According to the calculations of a conscientious writer whose theories, however, I do not fully accept, the average number of indigents in France is one pauper to twenty inhabitants. But immense differences are observable between the different parts of the kingdom. The department of the Nord, which is certainly the richest, the most populous, and the most advanced from all points of view, reckons close to a sixth of its population for whom charity is necessary. In the Creuse, the poorest and least industrial of all our departments, there is only one indigent to every fifty-eight inhabitants. In this statistical account, La Manche is listed as having one pauper for every twenty-six inhabitants.

I think that it is not impossible to give a reasonable explanation for this phenomenon. The effect that I have just pointed out is due to several general causes which it would take too long to examine thoroughly, but they can at least be indicated.

Here, to make myself clearly understood, I am compelled to return for a moment to the source of human societies. I will then go rapidly down the river of humanity to our own times.

We see men assembling for the first time. They come out of the forest, they are still savages; they associate not to enjoy life but in order to find the means of living. The object of their efforts is to find a refuge against the intemperance of the seasons and sufficient nourishment. Their imaginations do not go beyond these goods, and, if they obtain them without exertion, they consider themselves satisfied with their fate and slumber in their idle comfort. I have lived among the barbarous tribes of North America; I pitied them their destiny, but they do not find it at all a cruel one. Lying amidst the smoke of his cabin, covered with coarse clothes—the work of his hands or the fruit of the hunt—the Indian looks with pity on our arts, considering the

refinements of our civilisation a tiresome and shameful subjuga-
tion. They envy us only our weapons.

Having arrived at this first age of societies, men therefore still
have very few desires, they feel hardly any needs but ones
analogous to those of animals; they have merely discovered the
means of satisfying them with the least effort through social
organisation. Before agriculture is known to them they live by the
hunt. From the moment that they have learned the art of
producing harvests from the earth, they become farmers.
Everyone then reaps enough to feed himself and his children
from the field which happens to fall into his hands. Private
property is created, and with it enters the most active element of
progress.

From the moment that men possess land, they settle. They find
in the cultivation of the soil abundant resources against hunger.
Assured of a livelihood, they begin to glimpse that there are other
sources of pleasure in human existence than the satisfaction of
the more imperious needs of life.

While men were wanderers and hunters, inequality was unable
to insinuate itself among them in any permanent manner. There
existed no outward sign which could permanently establish the
superiority of one man and above all of one family over another
man or family; and this sign, had it existed, could not have been
transmitted to his children. But from the moment that landed
property was recognised and men had converted the vast forests
into fertile cropland and rich pasture, from this moment,
individuals arose who accumulated more land than they required
to feed themselves and so perpetuated property in the hands of
their progeny. Henceforth abundance exists; with superfluity
comes the taste for pleasures other than the satisfaction of the
crudest physical needs.

The origins of almost all aristocracies should be sought in this
social stage. While some men are already familiar with the art of
concentrating wealth, power, and almost all the intellectual and
material pleasures of life in the hands of a small minority, the
half-savage crowd is still unaware of the secret of diffusing
comfort and liberty among all. At this stage of human history
men have already abandoned the crude and proud virtues born
of the forest. They have lost the advantages of barbarism without
acquiring those of civilisation. Tilling the land is their only

resource, and they are ignorant of the means of protecting the fruits of their labours. Placed between a savage independence that they no longer desire, and a political and civil liberty that they do not yet understand, they are defenceless against violence and deceit, and seem prepared to submit to every kind of tyranny provided that they are allowed to live or rather vegetate in their fields.

At this point landed property is concentrated without restriction; power is also concentrated in a few hands. War menaces the private property of each citizen instead of endangering the political condition of peoples, as happens at present. The spirit of conquest, which has been the father and mother of all durable aristocracies, is strengthened and inequality reaches its extreme limits.

The barbarians who invaded the Roman Empire at the end of the fourth century were savages who had perceived what landed property could offer and who wanted to monopolize its advantages. The majority of the Roman provinces that they attacked were populated by men already long accustomed to farming, whose habits were softened by peaceful agricultural occupations, but among whom civilisation had not yet made great enough progress to enable them to counteract the primitive boldness of their enemies. Victory gave the barbarians not only the government but the property of the third estate. The cultivator became a tenant-farmer instead of an owner. Inequality was legalised; it became a right after having been a fact. Feudal society was organised and the Middle Ages were born. If one looks closely at what has happened to the world since the beginning of societies, it is easy to see that equality is prevalent only at the historical poles of civilisation. Savages are equal because they are equally weak and ignorant. Very civilised men can all become equal because they all have at their disposal similar means of attaining comfort and happiness. Between these two extremes is found inequality of conditions, wealth, knowledge—the power of the few, the poverty, ignorance, and weakness of all the rest.

Able and learned writers have already studied the Middle Ages, others are still working at it, among them the secretary of the Academic Society of Cherbourg. I therefore leave the enormous task of doing so to men more qualified than I am.

At this point, I want to examine only a corner of that immense tableau of the feudal centuries. In the twelfth century, what has since been called the 'third estate' did not yet exist. The population was divided into only two categories. On the one hand were those who cultivated the soil without possessing it; on the other, those who possessed the soil without cultivating it.

As for the first group of the population, I imagine that in certain regards its fate was less deserving of pity than that of the common people of our era. These men were in a situation like that of our colonial slaves, although they played their role with more liberty, dignity, and morality. Their means of subsistence was almost always assured; the interest of the master coincided with their own on this point. Limited in their desires as well as in their power, without anxiety about a present or a future which was not theirs to choose, they enjoyed a kind of vegetative happiness. It is as difficult for the very civilised man to understand its charm as it is to deny its existence.

The other class presented the opposite picture. Among these men hereditary leisure was combined with continuous and assured abundance. I am far from believing, however, that even within this privileged class the pursuit of pleasure was as preponderant as is generally supposed. Luxury without comfort can easily exist in a still half-barbarous nation. Comfort presupposes a numerous class all of whose members work together to render life milder and easier. But, in the period under discussion, the number of those not totally absorbed in self-preservation was extremely small. Their life was brilliant, ostentatious, but not comfortable. One ate with one's fingers on silver or engraved steel plates, clothes were lined with ermine and gold, and linen was unknown; the walls of their dwellings dripped with moisture, and they sat in richly sculptured wooden chairs before immense hearths where entire trees were consumed without diffusing sufficient heat around them. I am convinced that there is not a provincial town today whose more fortunate inhabitants do not have more true comforts of life in their homes and do not find it easier to satisfy the thousand needs created by civilisation than the proudest medieval baron. If we look carefully at the feudal centuries, we will discover in fact that the great majority of the population lived almost without needs and that the remainder felt only a small number of them. The land was enough for all needs. Subsistence was universal; comfort unheard of.

It was necessary to establish this point of departure in order to make clear what follows.

As time passes, the population which cultivates the soil acquires new tastes. The satisfaction of the basic necessities is no longer sufficient. The peasant, without leaving his fields, wants to be better housed and clothed. He has seen life's comforts and he wants them. On the other hand, the class which lived off the land without cultivating the soil extends the range of its pleasures; these become less ostentatious, but more complex, more varied. Thousands of needs unknown to the medieval nobles stimulate their descendants. A great number of men who lived on the land and from the land leave their fields and find their livelihood by working to satisfy these newly discovered needs. Agriculture which was everyone's occupation is now only that of the majority. Alongside those who live in leisure from the productivity of the soil arises a numerous class who live by working at a trade but without cultivating the soil.

Each century, as it emerges from the hand of the Creator, extends the range of thought, increases the desires and the power of man. The poor and the rich, each in his sphere, conceive of new enjoyments which were unknown to their ancestors. In order to satisfy these new needs, which the cultivation of the soil cannot meet, a portion of the population leaves agricultural labour each year for industry.

If one carefully considers what has happened in Europe over several centuries, it is certain that proportionately as civilisation progressed, a large population displacement occurred. Men left the plow for the shuttle and the hammer; they moved from the thatched cottage to the factory. In doing so, they were obeying the immutable laws which govern the growth of organised societies. One can no more assign an end to this movement than impose limits on human perfectibility. The limits of both are known only by God.

What has been, what is the consequence of this gradual and irresistible movement that we have just described? An immense number of new commodities has been introduced into the world; the class which had remained in agriculture found at its disposal a multitude of luxuries previously unknown. The life of the farmer became more pleasant and comfortable; the life of the great proprietor more varied and more ornate; comfort was available to the majority. But these happy results have not been obtained without a necessary cost.

I have stated that in the Middle Ages comfort could be found nowhere, but life everywhere. This sentence sums up what follows. When almost the entire population lived off the soil great poverty and rude manners could exist, but man's most pressing needs were satisfied. It is only rarely that the earth cannot provide enough to appease the pangs of hunger for anyone who will sweat for it. The population was therefore impoverished but it lived. Today the majority is happier but it would always be on the verge of dying of hunger if public support were lacking.

Such a result is easy to understand. The farmer produces basic necessities. The market may be better or worse, but it is almost guaranteed; and if an accidental cause prevents the disposal of agricultural produce, this produce at least gives its harvester something to live on and permits him to wait for better times.

The worker, on the contrary, speculates on secondary needs which a thousand causes can restrict and important events completely eliminate. However bad the times or the market, each man must have a certain minimum of nourishment or he languishes and dies, and he is always ready to make extraordinary sacrifices in order to obtain this. But unfortunate circumstances can lead the population to deny itself certain pleasures to which it would ordinarily be attracted. It is the taste and demand for these pleasures which the worker counts on for a living. If they are lacking, no other resource remains to him. His own harvest is consumed, his fields are barren; should such a condition continue, his prospect is only misery and death.

I have spoken only of the case where the population restricts its needs. Many other causes can lead to the same effect: domestic overproduction, foreign competition, etc.

The industrial class which gives so much impetus to the well-being of others is thus much more exposed to sudden and irremediable evils. In the total fabric of human societies, I consider the industrial class as having received from God the special and dangerous mission of securing the material well-being of all others by its risks and dangers. The natural and irresistible movement of civilisation continuously tends to increase the comparative size of this class. Each year needs multiply and diversify, and with them grows the number of individuals who hope to achieve greater comfort by working to satisfy those new needs rather than by remaining occupied in agriculture. Contemporary statesmen would do well to consider this fact.

To this must be attributed what is happening within wealthy societies where comfort and indigence are more closely connected than elsewhere. The industrial class, which provides for the pleasures of the greatest number, is itself exposed to miseries that would be almost unknown if this class did not exist.

However, still other causes contribute to the gradual development of pauperism. Man is born with needs, and he creates needs for himself. The first class belongs to his physical constitution, the second to habit and education. I have shown that at the outset men had scarcely anything but natural needs, seeking only to live; but in proportion as life's pleasures have become more numerous, they have become habits. These in turn have finally become almost as necessary as life itself. I will cite the habit of smoking, because tobacco is a luxury which has even permeated the wilderness and which has created an artificial pleasure among the savages that they must obtain at any price. Tobacco is almost as indispensable to the Indian as nourishment; he is apt to resort to begging when he lacks either. Here is a cause of beggary unknown to his forefathers. What I have said of tobacco is applicable to a multitude of objects which could not be sacrificed in civilised life. The more prosperous a society is, the more diversified and more durable become the enjoyments of the greatest number, the more they simulate true necessity through habit and imitation. Civilised man is therefore infinitely more exposed to the vicissitudes of destiny than savage man. What happens to the second only from time to time and in particular circumstances, occurs regularly to the first. Along with the range of his pleasures he has expanded the range of his needs and leaves himself more open to the hazard of fortune. Thus the English poor appear almost rich to the French poor; and the latter are so regarded by the Spanish poor. What the Englishman lacks has never been possessed by the Frenchman. And so it goes as one descends the social scale. Among very civilised peoples, the lack of a multitude of things causes poverty; in the savage state, poverty consists only in not finding something to eat.

The progress of civilisation not only exposes men to many new misfortunes: it even brings society to alleviate miseries which are not even thought about in less civilised societies. In a country where the majority is ill-clothed, ill-housed, ill-fed, who thinks of giving clean clothes, healthy food, comfortable quarters to the poor? The majority of the English, having all these things, regard their absence as a frightful misfortune; society believes itself bound to come to the aid of those who lack them, and cures evils which are not even recognised elsewhere. In England, the average standard of living a man can hope for in the course of his life is higher than in any other country of the world. This greatly facilitates the extension of pauperism in that kingdom.

If all these reflections are correct it is easy to see that the richer a nation is, the more the number of those who appeal to public charity must multiply, since two very powerful causes tend to that result. On the one hand, among these nations, the most insecure class continuously grows. On the other hand, needs infinitely expand and diversify, and the chance of being exposed to some of them becomes more frequent each day.

We should not delude ourselves. Let us look calmly and quietly on the future of modern societies. We must not be intoxicated by the spectacle of its greatness; let us not be discouraged by the sight of its miseries. As long as the present movement of civilisation continues, the standard of living of the greatest number will rise; society will become more perfected, better informed; existence will be easier, milder, more embellished, and longer. But at the same time we must look forward to an increase of those who will need to resort to the support of all their fellow men to obtain a small part of these benefits. It will be possible to moderate this double movement; special national circumstances will precipitate or suspend its course; but no one can stop it. We must discover the means of attenuating those inevitable evils which are already apparent.

Part II

THERE ARE two kinds of welfare. One leads each individual, according to his means, to alleviate the evils he sees around him. This type is as old as the world; it began with human misfortune. Christianity made a divine virtue of it, and called it charity. The other, less instinctive, more reasoned, less emotional, and often more powerful, leads society to concern itself with the misfortunes of its members and is ready systematically to alleviate their sufferings. This type is born of Protestantism and has developed only in modern societies. The first type is a private virtue; it escapes social action; the second on the contrary is produced and regulated by society. It is therefore with the second that we must be especially concerned.

At first glance there is no idea which seems more beautiful and grander than that of public charity. Society is continually examining itself, probing its wounds, and undertaking to cure them. At the same time that it assures the rich the enjoyment of their wealth, society guarantees the poor against excessive misery. It asks some to give of their surplus in order to allow others the basic necessities. This is certainly a moving and elevating sight.

How does it happen that experience destroys some of these beautiful illusions? The only country in Europe which has systematized and applied the theories of public charity on a grand scale is England. At the time of the religious revolution under Henry VIII, which changed the face of England, almost all the charitable foundations of the kingdom were suppressed; and since their wealth became the possession of the nobles and was not at all distributed among the common people, the poor remained as numerous as before while the means of providing for them were partly destroyed. The numbers of the poor therefore grew beyond measure, and Elizabeth, Henry's daughter, struck by the appalling miseries of the people, wished to substitute an annual levy furnished by the local governments for the sharply reduced alms-giving caused by the suppression of the convents.

A law promulgated in the forty-third year of that ruler's reign[3] declared that, in each parish, overseers of the poor would be chosen, and that these overseers would have the right to tax the inhabitants in order to feed disabled indigents, and to furnish work for the others.

As time passed, England was increasingly led to adopt the principle of legal charity. Pauperism grew more rapidly in Great Britain than anywhere else. Some general and some special causes produced this unfortunate result. The English have surpassed the other nations of Europe in civilised living. All the observations that I made before are applicable to them; but there are others which relate to that country alone.

The English industrial class not only provides for the necessities and pleasures of the English people, but of a large part of humanity. Its prosperity or its miseries therefore depend not only on what happens in Great Britain but in a way on every event under the sun. When an inhabitant of the Indies reduces his expenditure or cuts back on his consumption, it is an English manufacturer who suffers. England is therefore the country in the world where the agricultural labourer is most forcefully attracted towards industrial labour and finds himself most exposed to the vicissitudes of fortune. In the past century an event has occurred which, looking at the rest of the world's development, can be viewed as phenomenal. For a hundred years landed property has been breaking up throughout the known world; in England it continues to concentrate. Medium-sized holdings disappear into vast domains. Large-scale agriculture succeeds small-scale cultivation. One could offer some interesting observations on this subject, but it would divert me from my chosen topic: the fact must suffice—it is a constant. The result is that while the agricultural worker is moved by his interest to abandon the plough and to move into industry, he is in a way thrust in the same direction in spite of himself by the agglomeration of landed property. Comparatively speaking, infinitely fewer workers are required to work a large estate than a small field. The land fails him and industry beckons in this double movement. Of the twenty-five million people of Great Britain, no more than nine million are involved in agriculture. Fourteen million, or close to two-thirds, make their perilous way in commerce and industry.[4] Thus pauperism was bound to grow more quickly in England than in countries whose civilisation might have been equal to that of the English. Once having admitted the principle of legal charity, England has not been able to dispense with it. For two hundred years English legislation for the poor has revealed itself as nothing more than an extended development of the Elizabethan laws. Almost two and a half centuries have passed since the principle of legal charity was fully embraced by our neighbours, and one may now judge the fatal consequences which flowed from the adoption of this principle. Let us examine them successively.

Since the poor have an absolute right to the help of society, and have a public administration organised to provide it everywhere, one can observe in a Protestant country the immediate rebirth and generalisation of all the abuses with which its reformers rightly reproached some Catholic countries. Man, like all socially organised beings, has a natural passion for idleness. There are, however, two incentives to work: the need to live and the desire to improve the conditions of life. Experience has proven that the majority of men can be sufficiently motivated to work only by the first of these incentives. The second is only effective with a small minority. Well, a charitable institution indiscriminately open to all those in need, or a law which gives all the poor a right to public aid, whatever the origin of their poverty, weakens or destroys the first stimulant and leaves only the second intact. The English peasant, like the Spanish peasant, if he does not feel the deep desire to better the position into which he has been born, and to raise himself out of his misery (a feeble desire which is easily crushed in the majority of men) —the peasant of both countries, I maintain, has no interest in working, or, if he works, has no interest in saving. He therefore remains idle or thoughtlessly squanders the fruits of his labours. Both these countries, by different causal patterns, arrive at the same result: the most generous, the most active, the most industrious part of the nation, which devotes its resources to furnishing the means of existence for those who do nothing or who make bad use of their labour.

We are certainly far from that beautiful and seductive theory that I expounded above. Is it possible to escape the fatal consequences of a good principle? For myself I consider them inevitable. Here I might be interrupted by a rejoinder: You assume that, whatever its cause, misery will be alleviated; you add that public assistance will relieve the poor of the obligation to work. This states as a fact something questionable. What is to prevent society from inquiring into the causes of the need before giving assistance? Why could work not be imposed as a condition on the able-bodied indigent who asks for public pity? I reply that some English laws have used the idea of these palliatives; but they have failed, and understandably so.

Nothing is so difficult to distinguish as the nuances which separate unmerited misfortune from an adversity produced by vice. How many miseries are simultaneously the result of both these causes! What profound knowledge must be presumed about the character of each man and of the circumstances in which he has lived, what knowledge, what sharp discernment, what cold and inexorable reason! Where will you find the magistrate who will have the conscience, the time, the talent, the means of devoting himself to such an examination? Who would dare to let a poor man die of hunger because it's his own fault that he is dying? Who will hear his cries and reason about his vices? Even personal interest is restrained when confronted by the sight of other men's misery. Would the interest of the public treasury really prove to be more successful? And if the overseer's heart were unconcerned with such emotions, which are appealing even when misguided, would he remain indifferent to fear? Who, being judge of the joy or suffering, life or death, of a large segment of his fellow men, of its most dissolute, its most turbulent, its crudest segment, who would not shrink before the exercise of such terrible power? And if any of these intrepid beings can be found, how many will there be? In any event such functions can only be exercised with a restricted territory. A large number must be delegated to do so. The English have been obliged to put overseers in every parish. What inevitably follows from all this? Poverty is verified, the causes of poverty remain uncertain: the first is a patent fact, the second is proved by an always debatable process of reasoning. Since public aid is only indirectly harmful to society, while the refusal of aid instantly hurts the poor and the overseer himself, the overseer's choice cannot be in doubt. The laws may declare that only innocent poverty will be relieved; practice will alleviate all poverty. I will present plausible arguments for the second point, equally based on experience.

We would like work to be the price of relief. But, first, is there always public work to be done? Is it equally spread over the whole country in such a way that you never see a good deal of work to be done with few people to do it in one district and in another many indigents to be helped but little work to be undertaken? If this difficulty is present at all times, doesn't it become insurmountable when, as a consequence of the progressive development of civilisation, of population growth, of the effect of the Poor Law itself, the proportion of indigents, as in England, reaches a sixth, some say a quarter, of the total population?

But even supposing that there would always be work to do, who will take responsibility for determining its urgency, supervising its execution, setting the price? That man, the overseer, aside from the qualities of a great magistrate, will therefore also possess the talents, the energy, the special knowledge of a good industrial entrepreneur. He will find in the feeling of duty alone what self-interest itself would be powerless to create—the courage to force the most inactive and vicious part of the population into sustained and productive effort. Would it be wise to delude ourselves? Pressured by the needs of the poor, the overseer will impose make-work, or even—as is almost always the case in England—pay wages without demanding labour. Laws must be made for men and not in terms of a perfect world which cannot be sustained by human nature, nor of models which it offers only very occasionally.

Any measure which establishes legal charity on a permanent basis and gives it an administrative form thereby creates an idle and lazy class, living at the expense of the industrial and working class. This, at least, is its inevitable consequence if not the immediate result. It reproduces all the vices of the monastic system, minus the high ideals of morality and religion which often went along with it. Such a law is a bad seed planted in the legal structure. Circumstances, as in America, can prevent the seed from developing rapidly, but they cannot destroy it, and if the present generation escapes its influence, it will devour the well-being of generations to come.

If you closely observe the condition of populations among whom such legislation has long been in force you will easily discover that the effects are not less unfortunate for morality than for public prosperity, and that it depraves men even more than it impoverishes them.

There is nothing which, generally speaking, elevates and sustains the human spirit more than the idea of rights. There is something great and virile in the idea of right which removes from any request its suppliant character, and places the one who claims it on the same level as the one who grants it. But the right of the poor to obtain society's help is unique in that instead of elevating the heart of the man who exercises it, it lowers him. In countries where legislation does not allow for such an opportunity, the poor man, while turning to individual charity, recognises, it is true, his condition of inferiority in relation to the rest of his fellow men; but he recognizes it secretly and temporarily. From the moment that an indigent is inscribed on the poor list of his parish, he can certainly demand relief, but what is the achievement of this right if not a notarised manifestation of misery, of weakness, of misconduct on the part of its recipient? Ordinary rights are conferred on men by reason of some personal advantage acquired by them over their fellow men. This other kind is accorded by reason of a recognised inferiority. The first is a clear statement of superiority; the second publicises inferiority and legalises it. The more extensive and the more secure ordinary rights are, the more honour they confer; the more permanent and extended the right to relief is, the more it degrades.

The poor man who demands alms in the name of the law is, therefore, in a still more humiliating position than the indigent who asks pity of his fellow men in the name of He who regards all men from the same point of view and who subjects rich and poor to equal laws.

But this is still not all: individual alms-giving established valuable ties between the rich and the poor. The deed itself involves the giver in the fate of the one whose poverty he has undertaken to alleviate. The latter, supported by aid which he had no right to demand and which he may have had no hope of getting, feels inspired by gratitude. A moral tie is established between those two classes whose interests and passions so often conspire to separate them from each other, and although divided by circumstance they are willingly reconciled. This is not the case with legal charity. The latter allows the alms to persist, but removes its morality. The law strips the man of wealth of a part of his surplus without consulting him and he sees the poor man only as a greedy stranger invited by the legislator to share his wealth. The poor man, on the other hand, feels no gratitude for a benefit which no one can refuse him and which could not satisfy him in any case. Public alms guarantee life, but do not make it happier or more comfortable than individual alms-giving; legal charity does not thereby eliminate wealth or poverty in society. One class still views the world with fear and loathing while the other regards its misfortune with despair and envy. Far from uniting these two rival nations, who have existed since the beginning of the world and who are called the rich and the poor, into a single people, it breaks the only link which could be established between them. It ranges each one under a banner, tallies them, and, bringing them face to face, prepares them for combat.

I have said that the inevitable result of public charity was to perpetuate idleness among the majority of the poor and to provide for their leisure at the expense of those who work.

If the idleness of the rich, an hereditary idleness, merited by work or by services, an idleness immersed in public consideration, supported by psychological complacency, inspired by intellectual pleasures, moralised by mental exercise—if this idleness, I say, has produced so many vices, what will come of a degraded idleness obtained by baseness, merited by misconduct, enjoyed in ignominy? It becomes tolerable only in proportion to the extent that the soul subjects itself to all this corrupting and degrading.

What can be expected from a man whose position cannot improve, since he has lost the respect of his fellow men which is the precondition of all progress, whose lot could not become worse, since, being reduced to the satisfaction of his most pressing needs, he is assured that they will always be satisfied? What course of action is left to the conscience or to human activity in a being so limited, who lives without hope and without fear? He looks at the future as an animal does. Absorbed in the present and the ignoble and transient pleasures it affords, his brutalised nature is unaware of the determinants of its destiny.

Read all the books on pauperism written in England, study the inquiries ordered by the British Parliament, look at the discussions which have taken place in the Lords and Commons on this difficult question. They boil down to a single deafening cry—the degraded condition into which the lower classes have fallen! The number of illegitimate children and criminals grows rapidly and continuously, the indigent population is limitless, the spirit of foresight and of saving becomes more and more alien to the poor. While throughout the rest of the nation education spreads, morals improve, tastes become more refined, manners more polished—the indigent remains motionless, or rather he goes backwards. He could be described as reverting to barbarism. Amidst the marvels of civilisation, he seems to emulate savage man in his ideas and his inclinations.

Legal charity affects the pauper's freedom as much as his morality. This is easily proved. When local governments are rigorously obligated to aid the indigent, they necessarily owe relief only to the poor who reside in their jurisdiction. This is the only fair way of equalising the public burden which results from the law, and of proportioning it to the means of those who must bear it. Since individual charity is almost unknown in a country of organised public charity, anyone whose misfortunes or vices have made him incapable of earning a living is condemned, under pain of death, to remain in the place of his birth. If he leaves, he moves through enemy country. The private interest within the parish, infinitely more active and powerful than the best organised national police could be, notes his arrival, dogs his every step, and, if he wants to establish a new residence, informs the public authority who takes him to the boundary line. Through their Poor Laws, the English have immobilised a sixth of their population. They have bound it to the earth like the medieval peasantry. Then, man was forced against his will to stay on the land where he was born. Legal charity keeps him from even wishing to move. That is the only difference between the systems. The English have gone further. They have reaped even more disastrous consequences from the principle of public welfare. The English parishes are so dominated by the fear that an indigent person might be placed on their rolls and acquire residency, that when a stranger whose clothes do not clearly indicate wealth temporarily settles among them, or when an unexpected misfortune suddenly strikes him, the municipal authorities immediately ask him to post bond against possible indigence, and if the stranger cannot furnish this security, he must leave.

Thus legal charity has not only taken freedom of movement from the English poor, but also from those who are threatened by poverty.

I know of no better way to complete this sad picture than by reproducing the following fragment from my notes on England. I travelled through Great Britain in 1833. Others were struck by the imposing prosperity of the country. I myself pondered the secret unrest which was visibly at work among all its inhabitants. I thought that great misery must be hidden beneath that brilliant mask of prosperity which Europe admires. This idea led me to pay particular attention to pauperism, that hideous and enormous sore which is attached to a healthy and vigorous body.

I was staying at the house of a great proprietor in the south of England at the time when the justices of the peace assemble to pass judgment on the suits brought to court by the poor against the parish, or by the parishes against the poor. My host was a justice of the peace, and I regularly accompanied him to court. I find in my travel notes this portrait of the first sitting that I attended. It gives a short concise summary and clarifies everything said before. I am reproducing it with scrupulous exactness in order to render a true picture.

The first individual who comes before the justices of the peace is an old man. His face is honest and ruddy, he wears a wig and is dressed in excellent black clothes. He seems like a man of property. However, he approaches the bar and passionately protests against the parish administration's injustice. This man is a pauper, and his share of public charity has just been unjustly diminished. The case is adjourned in order to hear the parish administrators.

After this hale and petulant old man comes a pregnant young woman whose clothes bear witness to recent poverty and who bears the marks of suffering on her withered features. She explains that some time ago her husband set out on a sea voyage, that since then she has received neither assistance nor news from him. She claims public charity but the overseer of the poor hesitates to give it to her. This woman's father-in-law is a well-to-do merchant. He lives in the very city where the court is sitting, and it is hoped too, that in the absence of his son, he will certainly want to take responsibility for the maintainance of his daughter-in-law. The justices of the peace summon this man; but he refuses to fulfill the duties imposed on him by nature and not by law. The judges insist. They try to create remorse or compassion in this man's egoistic soul. Their efforts fail, and the parish is sentenced to pay the requested relief.

After this poor abandoned woman come five or six big and vigorous men. They are in the bloom of youth, their bearing is resolute and almost insulting. They lodge a complaint against their village administrators who refuse to give them work, or, for lack of work, relief.

The administrators reply that at the moment the parish is not carrying out any public work; and gratuitous relief is not required they say, because the plaintiffs could easily find jobs with private individuals if they wanted to.

Lord X [Radnor], with whom I had come, tells me, 'you have just seen in microcosm part of the numerous abuses which the Poor Law produces. That old man who came first quite probably has the means to live, but he thinks that he has the right to demand that he be supported in comfort, and he does not blush to claim public charity, which has lost all of its afflicting and humiliating character in the people's eyes. That young woman, who seems honest and unfortunate, would certainly be helped by her father-in-law if the Poor Law did not exist; but interest silences the cry of shame within him and he unloads a debt on the public that he alone ought to discharge. As for those young people who appeared last, I know them, they live in my village. They are very dangerous citizens and indeed bad subjects. They quickly squander the money they earn in taverns because they know they will be given relief. As you see, they appeal to us at the first difficulty caused by their own shortcomings.'

The sitting continues. A young woman comes before the bar, followed by the overseer of the poor of her parish. She approaches without showing the slightest sign of hesitation, her gaze not at all lowered by a sense of shame. The overseer accuses her of having had the baby she is carrying through unlawful intercourse.

She freely admits this. As she is indigent and if the father remained unknown the illegitimate child would become a public charge along with its mother, the overseer calls on her to name the father; the court puts her under oath. She names a neighbourhood peasant. The latter, who is present among the audience, very obligingly admits the accuracy of the fact, and the justices of the peace sentence him to support the child. The father and the mother retire and the incident does not excite the least emotion in an audience accustomed to such scenes.

After this young woman comes another. She comes willingly. She approaches the judges with the same shameless indifference shown by the first. She declares herself pregnant and names the father of the unborn child. This man is absent. The court adjourns the case in order to have him summoned.

Lord X tells me: 'Here again are the harmful effects produced by the same laws. The most direct consequence of the Poor Laws is to make the public responsible for the support of deserted children who are the neediest of all indigents. Out of this comes the parish's desire to free themselves of the duty to support illegitimate children whose parents would be in a position to nurture them. Out of this also come the paternity suits instigated by the parishes, proof of which is left to the woman. For what other kind of proof can one delude oneself into expecting in such a case? By obliging the parishes to become responsible for illegitimate children and permitting the paternity suits in order to ease this crushing weight, we have facilitated the misconduct of lower-class women as much as we could. Illegitimate pregnancy must almost always improve their material condition. If the father of the child is rich, they can unload the responsibility of raising the fruit of their common blunder on him; if he is poor, they entrust this responsibility to society. The relief granted to them in either way exceeds the expenses caused by the infant. So they thrive from their very vices, and it often happens that a woman who has become a mother several times over concludes a more advantageous marriage than the young virgin who has only her virtues to offer. They have a dowry of infamy.'[5]

I repeat that I wanted to change nothing from this passage in my diary. I have reproduced it exactly, because it seemed to me that it rendered the impressions that I would have the reader share with truth and simplicity.

Since the time of my English journey the Poor Law has been modified. Many Englishmen flatter themselves that these changes will exercise great influence on the indigents' future, on their morality, and on their number. I would like to be able to share these hopes, but I cannot do so. In the new law the present-day English have again reaffirmed the principle introduced two hundred years ago by Elizabeth. Like that ruler, they have imposed on society the obligation of feeding the poor. That is quite enough. All the abuses that I have tried to describe are contained in it, just as the biggest oak is contained in the acorn that a child can hide in its hand. It needs only time to develop and grow. To want to create a law which regularly, permanently, and uniformly relieves indigency without also increasing the indigent population, without increasing their laziness along with their needs, and their idleness with their vices, is to plant an acorn and to be stunned when a stem appears, followed by leaves, flowers, and fruits, which in turn will one day produce a whole forest from the bowels of the earth.

I am certainly far from wanting to put the most natural, the most beautiful, and the most holy of virtues on trial. But I think that there is no principle, however good, whose every consequence can be regarded as good. I think that beneficence must be a manly and reasoned virtue, not a weak and unreflecting inclination. It is necessary to do what is most useful to the receiver, not what pleases the giver, to do what best serves the welfare of the majority, not what rescues the few. I can conceive of beneficence only in this way. Any other way it is still a sublime instinct, but it no longer seems to me worthy of the name of virtue.

I recognize that individual charity almost always produces useful results. It devotes itself to the greatest miseries, it seeks out misfortune without publicity, and it silently and spontaneously repairs the damage. It can be observed wherever there are unfortunates to be helped. It grows with suffering. And yet, it cannot be unthinkingly relied on, because a thousand accidents can delay or halt its operation. One cannot be sure of finding it, and it is not aroused by every cry of pain.

I admit that by regulating relief, charitable persons in association could infuse individual philanthropy with more activity and power. I recognize not only the utility but the necessity of public charity applied to inevitable evils such as the helplessness of infancy, the decrepitude of old age, sickness, insanity. I even admit its temporary usefulness in times of public calamities which God sometimes allows to slip from his hand, proclaiming his anger to the nations. State alms are then as spontaneous as unforeseen, as temporary as the evil itself.

I even understand that public charity which opens free schools for the children of the poor and gives intelligence the means of acquiring the basic physical necessities through labour.

But I am deeply convinced that any permanent, regular, administrative system whose aim will be to provide for the needs of the poor, will breed more miseries than it can cure, will deprave the population that it wants to help and comfort, will in time reduce the rich to being no more than the tenant-farmers of the poor, will dry up the sources of savings, will stop the accumulation of capital, will retard the development of trade, will benumb human industry and activity, and will culminate by bringing about a violent revolution in the State, when the number of those who receive alms will have become as large as those who give it, and the indigent, no longer being able to take from the impoverished rich the means of providing for his needs, will find it easier to plunder them of all their property at one stroke than to ask for their help.

Let us summarize in a few words. The progressive movement of modern civilisation will gradually and in a roughly increasing proportion raise the number of those who are forced to turn to charity. What remedy can be applied to such evils? Legal alms comes to mind first—legal alms in all forms—sometimes unconditional, sometimes hidden in the disguise of a wage. Sometimes it is accidental and temporary, at other times regular and permanent. But intensive investigation quickly demonstrates that this remedy, which seems both so natural and so effective, is a very dangerous expedient. It affords only a false and momentary sop to individual suffering, and however used it inflames society's sores. We are left with individual charity. It can produce only useful results. Its very weakness is a guarantee against dangerous consequences. It alleviates many miseries and breeds none. But individual charity seems quite weak when faced with the progressive development of the industrial classes and all the evils which civilisation joins to the inestimable goods it produces. It was sufficient for the Middle Ages, when religious enthusiasm gave it enormous energy, and when its task was less difficult; could it be sufficient today when the burden is heavy and when its forces are so weakened? Individual charity is a powerful agency that must not be despised, but it would be imprudent to rely on it. It is but a single means and cannot be the only one. Then what is to be done? In what direction can we look? How can we mitigate what we can foresee, but not cure?

Up to this point I have examined the financial approach to poverty. But is this the only approach? After having considered alleviating evils, wouldn't it be useful to try to forestall them? Is there a way to prevent the rapid displacement of population, so that men do not leave the land and move into industry before the latter can easily respond to their needs? Can the total national wealth continue to increase without a part of those who produce this wealth having to curse the prosperity that they produce? Is it impossible to establish a more constant and exact relation between the production and consumption of manufactured goods? Can the working classes be helped to accumulate savings which would allow them to await a reversal of fortune in times of industrial calamity, without dying?

At this point my horizon widens on all sides. My subject grows. I see a path opening up, which I cannot follow at this moment. The present *Memoir*, too short for my subject, already exceeds the limits that I had thought it necessary to set for myself. The measures by which pauperism may be combatted preventively will be the object of a second work which I hope respectfully to submit next year to the Academic Society of Cherbourg.[6]

Notes

1 See Introduction, footnote on pp. 3-4.

2 Adriano Balbi, author of *Essai Statistique sur le Royaume de Portugal et d'Algarve comparé aux autres états de l'Europe*, Paris, 1822.

3 Tocqueville's note: See (1) *Blackstone*, Bk. I, Chapter IV; (2) The principal results of the enquiry made in 1833 on the condition of the poor, contained in the book entitled *Extracts from the Information Received by His Majesty's Commissioners as to the Administration and Operation of the Poor-laws*; (3) *The Report of the Poor-law Commissioners*; (4) and finally the law of 1834 which was the result of all these efforts.

4 Tocqueville's note: In France the industrial class as yet constitutes only a quarter of the population.

5 See Introduction p. 4.

6 See Introduction pp. 10-11.